ROSEN ✔ Verified

CURRENT ISSUES

FAKE NEWS

Jill Keppeler

ROSEN
PUBLISHING

New York

Published in 2021 by The Rosen Publishing Group, Inc.
29 East 21st Street, New York, NY 10010

First Edition

Editor: Amanda Vink
Book Design: Reann Nye

Photo Credits: Cover Mihajlo Maricic/EyeEm/Getty Images; series Art PinkPueblo/Shutterstock.com; p. 5 Carol Yepes/Moment/Getty Images; p. 7 simonkr/E+/Getty Images; p. 9 Hill Street Studios/DigitalVision/Getty Images; p. 11 Bettmann/Getty Images; p. 12, 13 GaudiLab/Shutterstock.com; p. 15 fizkes/iStock/Getty Images Plus/Getty Images; p. 16 George Rudy/Shutterstock.com; p. 17 II.studio/Shutterstock.com; p. 19 panuwat phimpha/Shutterstock.com; pp. 20–21 13_Phunkod/Shutterstock.com; pp. 22–23 Brocreative/Shutterstock.com; p. 25 Prostock-studio/Shutterstock.com; p. 27 SolStock/E+/Getty Images; p. 29 Andrey_Popov/Shutterstock.com; pp. 30–31 Bruce Glikas/FilmMagic/Getty Images; p. 33 The Washington Post/Getty Images; p. 34 Anton_Ivanov/Shutterstock.com; p. 35 Frederick M. Brown/Getty Images Entertainment/Getty Images; p. 37 mixetto/E+/Getty Images; p. 39 Take A Pix Media/Shutterstock.com; p. 41 Jeff Greenberg/ Universal Images Group/Getty Images; p. 43 Christopher Penler/Shutterstock.com; pp. 44–45 Mayur Kakade/Shutterstock.com.

Library of Congress Cataloging-in-Publication Data

Names: Keppeler, Jill, author.
Title: Fake news / Jill Keppeler.
Description: New York : Rosen Publishing, 2021. | Series: Rosen verified: current issues | Includes index.
Identifiers: LCCN 2019059509 | ISBN 9781499468342 (paperback) | ISBN 9781499468359 (library binding)
Subjects: LCSH: Fake news—United States. | Media literacy—United States.
Classification: LCC PN4888.F35 K47 2021 | DDC 070.4/3—dc23
LC record available at https://lccn.loc.gov/2019059509

Manufactured in the United States of America

CPSIA Compliance Information: Batch #BSR20. For Further Information contact Rosen Publishing, New York, New York at 1-800-237-9932.

Find us on

CONTENTS

THE TRUTH IS OUT THERE—ISN'T IT?

Fake news! For a handful of years now, it seems like those two little words have been tossed around a lot. In fact, they've been used so much that lots of people aren't sure what they really mean. Sometimes they're even used as a joke.

But there's really nothing funny about fake news. It can be a joke, but it can also be used to mislead, or trick, people about important things. It can spread so quickly that the truth can't catch up. Even stories that seem harmless can have bad effects. But if you know how to figure out the truth, you can act on it and make sure others know it too. That's a very valuable thing!

If you think something doesn't seem right about a story, there's a good chance you're correct.

WHAT'S NEWS?

News is **information**. It's something people want to know or should know. It's usually about something that happened recently. Your friend telling you that another friend is out of school that day is news. A report on TV about a fire near your home is news.

News doesn't have to be **serious**, though. A report about something fun happening in your city could be news too. News media are sources, or suppliers, of news. They gather and report it.

KINDS OF NEWS MEDIA

- Newspapers
- TV stations
- Websites
- Blogs
- Podcasts
- Magazines
- Radio programs

WHAT IS BREAKING NEWS?

Breaking news is news that's just happened or something that's happening right then. It's usually something important. People may still be learning about what happened. This means that early reports might be wrong or incomplete.

BREAKING NEWS

It's easy for people to become confused about breaking news stories. Things are still happening, and people are trying to figure it all out.

NEWS MEDIA AND DEMOCRACY

News adds to the open sharing of ideas and information. This is very important to a democracy. This kind of system is when the people of a country run their government or elect representatives. The more people know, the better decisions they can make when they vote.

"Congress shall make no law ... [taking away] the freedom of speech, or of the press."

— part of the First Amendment to the U.S. **Constitution**

Journalists also serve as watchdogs for society. They keep an eye on and report on what leaders are doing. They make sure leaders know what people think. They report about the whole world.

REPUBLIC OR DEMOCRACY?

Most of the people in the United States don't directly run the government. In the United States, we elect people to run it. This is a kind of democracy called a republic.

VOTE

It's very important to pay attention to real news from good sources. The more you know, the better your decisions will be.

NEWS IN THE UNITED STATES

The news media, especially newspapers, has a long history in our country. The U.S. Constitution protects, or keeps safe, its freedom of speech.

Journalists and news stories have changed the course of U.S. history for the better. They've uncovered problems and **corruption**. This doesn't mean they're perfect, though. Reporters can make mistakes. And, at one point, there weren't **ethics** standards for media. As new kinds of news media rise, we have to be careful about this. There are ways to decide what to trust.

The decision in the Zenger trial was very important. The **publisher** was arrested just because someone didn't like what he printed. That didn't mean what was printed wasn't true. He was found not **guilty**.

COLONIAL AND EARLY U.S. NEWSPAPERS TIMELINE

1690: The first newspaper in the future United States is printed in Boston.

1735: John Peter Zenger, publisher of the *New York Weekly Journal*, is found not guilty of **libel** because the articles he published were true.

1791: The states agree upon the Bill of Rights, including the First Amendment.

1850: There are more than 2,500 newspapers in the United States.

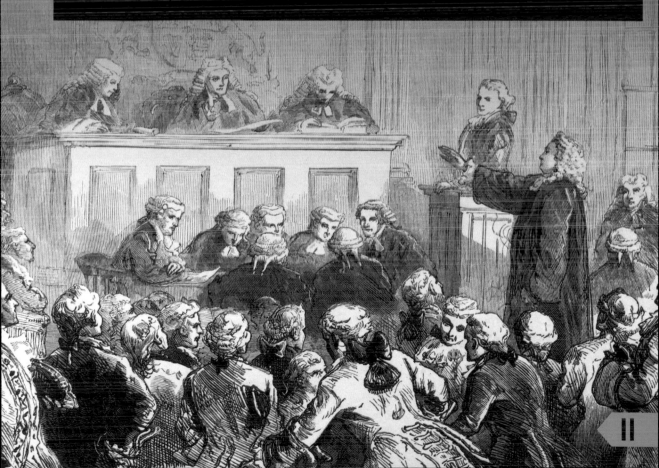

ETHICS AND NEWS

Good news sources follow ethics standards. These rules are meant to make sure news reports are **accurate** and fair. They also make sure news sources take **responsibility** for any mistakes. Mistakes can happen even with good sources! One way to see if a news source is trustworthy is to check to see if it has a code of ethics. Then see if it follows that code. Look to see if there's background about the news outlet and its leaders and workers too.

✓ VERIFIED

Society for Professional Journalists

The SPJ is a group of U.S. journalists that's existed since 1909. It has about 6,000 members. Many journalists use its ethics code.
www.spj.org/ethicscode.asp

Does your school have a newspaper or news website? Even school news media should have an ethics code.

ETHICS RULES

Here are a few items often on news ethics codes:
- Be accurate.
- Verify, or prove, information before you use it.
- Give background.
- Correct mistakes.
- Identify, or name, sources within reason.
- Keep news and **advertisements** separate.
- Don't take money or gifts to report things.
- Don't favor advertisers.

WHAT IS (AND ISN'T) FAKE NEWS

Fake news is something that looks like a real news story but isn't. It's usually created to fool or trick people. It might be meant to make them feel a certain way. Fake news stories often aim to make people angry or upset. However, sometimes people say something's fake news just because they don't like it. Maybe they don't want to believe it for some reason. However, this doesn't make it fake. Follow the facts and pay attention to them.

News stories that make you angry aren't always fake. But if something has that effect, you might want to read it again and think about it more.

SO MANY SOURCES

Perhaps the most important thing to look at when judging a news item is the source. Is it an established news source that's been around for a while? They can make mistakes, but they generally won't share fake news. Are there quotes in the story? Do they make sense? Did real people say the quotes? Is there a byline—the writer's name—on the story? Can you find more information about them? These are all good signs for a source.

You can check to see if other good news sources are reporting a story. There's strength in numbers.

WHERE IN THE WORLD?

Look to see if an online news source gives an address for its offices or other contact information. Is there any information you can prove about it? If not, be very **skeptical**.

🔒 www.courant.com

S OPINION SPORTS CTNOW COMMUNITY

Hartford Courant

PICS COURAN...   ...RS TAST

...PAPER CTNOW BEST OF HARTFORD

✅ VERIFIED

Oldest U.S. Newspaper

The *Hartford Courant* of Hartford, Connecticut, is the oldest newspaper in the United States. It was founded in 1764!

www.courant.com

RED FLAGS

There are many other things to look for when you think something might be fake news. Be sure the website address has the right ending, such as ".com" instead of ".com.co." Sometimes fake news sources will have sites that look a lot like real news sites. Are there a lot of spelling or writing mistakes? Real media sources have editors checking things. Do sentences have lots of exclamation points? Do they use too many capital letters? These are red flags that a story is fake.

FACT-CHECKING SITES

There are a number of good websites that can help you check something that seems like fake news. Some of the best are:

- Snopes.com
- Factcheck.org
- Politifact.com

CHECK THE LINKS

Sometimes fake news stories will have links that claim to back up their information. If you're questioning the story, check the links. They may have nothing to do with the so-called facts!

Fake news stories and websites count on people not looking a little deeper into what they say. Be skeptical!

BUT WHY?

It might seem odd or strange that fake news sources go to such lengths to trick and fool people. Why do they do it? There are a few reasons. Some sources make money off how many people go to their stories or sites. The wilder the story, the more people might click on it. And sometimes these sources want to make people think or feel—and then vote—a certain way. They try to make people mad or upset so they don't think.

Paul Horner

Paul Horner created many **hoaxes** and fake stories. Some are still shared on social media today. He even claimed his work was a reason for the Trump presidency. Horner died at age 38 in 2017.

THE 2016 ELECTION

Fake news can lead to real problems. Social media **bots** created in Russia have been one of these problems. They created and spread fake news around the 2016 U.S. presidential election. It likely affected the vote.

CONFIRMATION BIAS

A lot of fake news keeps spreading because people want to believe it. People like things that back up their beliefs. They don't like things that go against them, even if those facts are true. This is called confirmation bias. Imagine you really respect a certain basketball player. Wouldn't you be more likely to share a story that said something good about him—even if you weren't sure it was true? It works the other way too.

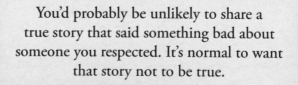

You'd probably be unlikely to share a true story that said something bad about someone you respected. It's normal to want that story not to be true.

FACT VS. OPINION

Another thing that gets people **confused** is opinion. Real news sources can share opinion pieces. However, these should always be clearly marked as opinion. Many times, they'll be in an editorial or **commentary** section. An opinion can't be untrue. Still, it can be based on things that are untrue. For example, you can say that you think your friend's favorite actor is a real jerk. But what if this opinion is based on a fake news story about them?

You can have an opinion on what kind of person an actor is, but what if it's not based on real information? Then it won't mean much.

SOCIAL MEDIA

Social media sites make keeping track of fake news even harder. Once people start sharing stories, it can get out of hand fast! Many times, people don't even take a closer look at links or sources. They just share the stories if they agree with them. Maybe they just look at the headline. Sometimes, people want to be the first to share something. Once something is trending on social media, it's hard to stop it.

SOCIAL MEDIA AND 2019 USERS

- Facebook (2.4 billion)
- YouTube (2 billion)
- WhatsApp (1.6 billion)
- Instagram (1 billion)
- Tumblr (472 million)
- Twitter (330 million)
- Snapchat (314 million)
- Pinterest (300 million)

People often share things online without reading more than the headline. This is a big way fake news spreads.

NOT REALLY A JOKE

In 2014, National Public Radio (NPR) shared a headline on its Facebook page. It said, "Why Doesn't America Read Anymore?" The link went to a webpage explaining that it was a joke. They asked readers to not comment on the post, but to like it. Many people commented without reading!

YOU WON'T BELIEVE WHAT HAPPENS NEXT!

Sometimes the idea behind fake news is to **lure** people into clicking on a link. This is often the case if the story doesn't have much actual news or **value**. Websites can make money based on how many people go there. Headlines are meant to capture interest and attention. These clickbait headlines are often misleading. They often take the reader to stories or items that aren't what was promised. They play on mystery, curiosity, or feelings.

YOU WON'T **BELIEVE** WHAT **HAPPENS NEXT!**

CLICK TO FIND OUT

Clickbait isn't always fake. It's often misleading, though.

IT'S VIRAL

When something spreads very quickly and widely on social media, we say it's gone viral. Often, this is pretty harmless. It might be just a funny meme or video or a cute photo. But news, real or fake, can go viral too. And the faster something spreads, the harder it is to stop if it's untrue or harmful. Think about this before you share something that might be fake. Check it out first. (Funny cat photos are probably still fine.)

Grumpy Cat's photo first went viral in 2012. After that, she became one of the internet's most famous cats.

WORTH A THOUSAND WORDS?

You can always trust a photo, right? Nope. It can be very easy to change a picture to show something that never really happened. People can also steal other people's photos online. They can say that they took them and lie about what they show. It can be hard to prove otherwise. Videos can be faked too. In fact, it's getting easier and easier to do this using apps and other tools. Still, there are signs you can watch for.

THINGS TO WATCH FOR

There are signs you can watch for in photos and videos to tell if they are true or not.

- Things that are only partly there
- Weird shadows or lighting
- Uneven edges around something
- **Flickering** in a video

"Deepfakes" are a way of changing the people in a video. The top photograph is from a real video of Facebook founder Mark Zuckerberg. The bottom photograph is from a deepfake video which shows Zuckerberg saying things he never said!

SATIRE SITES

Sometimes fake news stories and websites aren't really trying to trick people, but that doesn't mean people aren't fooled anyway! Satire is a kind of writing or art. It's supposed to be funny and point out things that are wrong or foolish. There are a number of well-known satire websites. Sometimes, people share things from these sites. When they do this without knowing or saying they're satire, it can confuse others. Good satire sites label their work. Watch for this!

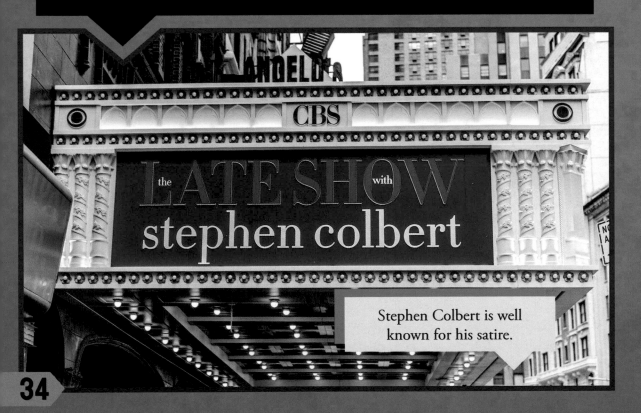

CBS

the LATE SHOW with
stephen colbert

Stephen Colbert is well known for his satire.

HISTORY OF SATIRE

Satire has been around for a very long time. It goes back to ancient Rome! There are satirical TV shows too. They include *The Daily Show with Trevor Noah* and *The Late Show with Stephen Colbert*.

✓ VERIFIED

America's "Finest" News Source

The Onion is one of the most famous satire websites. It started in 1988 as a print newspaper. Now it's online only.

theonion.com

SELLING YOU SOMETHING

Sponsored content isn't quite fake news. It can still mislead people. Sponsored content is sometimes called native advertising. It's when news sources run content that looks a lot like news. However, this content is paid for by an advertiser. It's meant to sell something or get information out for that advertiser. Even good news sources sometimes run sponsored content. However, it's part of basic journalism ethics to label it very clearly. There shouldn't be any confusion about it.

SIGNS OF SPONSORED CONTENT

- Labels such as "paid post" or "sponsored"
- Business or "staff" listed as the writer
- Links to a company's website

With sponsored content, a business pays for a spot in a news source. Real news stories are different. A trained reporter or editor decides something is worthy of being news.

MAYBE YOU WANT TO CHECK THAT OUT...

So what do you do if your friends or family members keep sharing fake news? Talk to them. Don't just tell them they're wrong. Even if they are, that probably won't work. Be nice and respectful. Tell them in person if you can. Show them real news sources and ways to check things online. And make sure you're not sharing fake news yourself! Your friends might think it's funny. Your family members—especially older ones— might not know better. But everyone can learn.

TAKE A BREAK

Sometimes, you just can't get people to believe you. If that happens, maybe you want to hide their posts or unfollow them for a bit. Maybe you can try again later.

There was a lot of fake news around during the 2016 election. People age 65 and older shared more fake news than any other group.

WHAT TO DO?

What else can you do about fake news? Well, it's important to support real news. Read, watch, or listen to different sources. Pay attention to sources besides social media. If you have one, support your local newspaper. It likely reports on things that no other news source does. Remember that fake news isn't just news you don't like or don't want to hear. Sometimes, news sources are there to tell you the truth even if the truth stinks!

WHY SUPPORT LOCAL NEWS?

- It tells you what local leaders are doing.

- It reports on local events and issues. These are things bigger news sources might not care about.

- It's more likely to report on things people your age are doing. Many local newspapers have a school reporter.

- It's more likely to report on local and school sports. This includes those you and your friends might be taking part in.

Have you ever been to a protest in your town or city? Local reporters often report on these things.

NEWSPAPER NUMBERS

More than 1,400 communities in the United States lost a local newspaper over the past 15 years. Newsroom jobs fell by 45 percent between 2004 and 2017.

IN THE FUTURE

People are looking at ways to fight fake news in the future. These include beating bots and teaching people to think about things in new ways. Still, new ways to trick people are created all the time, and that's alarming. It's going to be very important to be careful and skeptical. Fake news isn't just a joke. It can lead to real change in the world. And it might not be the kind of change you want to see.

TIPS FOR CRITICAL THINKING

Critical thinking is carefully thinking about facts before forming an opinion. Ask yourself these questions to fight fake news.

- Who created this?
- Why did they create it?
- Who's sending it out?
- How did it get my attention?
- Is something missing?

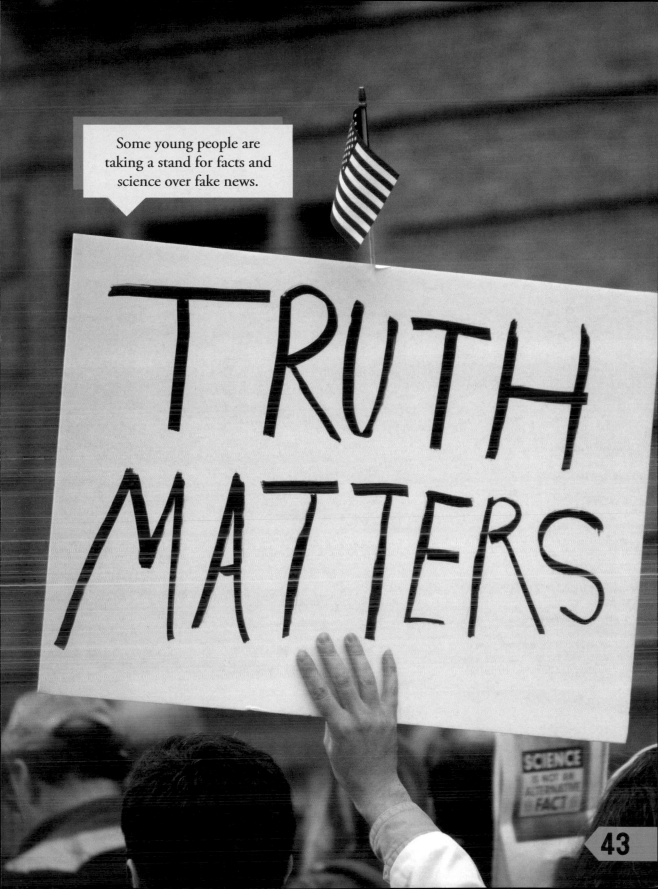

Some young people are taking a stand for facts and science over fake news.

TO TELL THE TRUTH

Fake news isn't new, but it's a big problem today. It causes people to believe lies over truth. It can lead to those people making bad choices based on those lies. It hurts real news and those who report it. And as long as fake news can make some people money and affect opinions, there will be those who make and spread it.

But you can fight it. The most important thing is not to spread fake news yourself. Understand what fake news is—and isn't. Think critically about things. Talk to your friends and family members. Truth is still truth, and facts are still facts. You can be part of the battle against fake news.

Stay informed. Fight fake news!

GLOSSARY

accurate: Free of mistakes.

advertisement: Something shown to sell a good or a service.

bot: A computer program that may seem to be a person on social media.

commentary: A written or spoken piece that provides opinion on something.

confused: Not clear.

constitution: The basic laws by which a country, state, or group is governed.

corruption: Dishonest or illegal behavior, especially by people in power.

ethics: Rules of behavior based on what is good and bad.

flicker: To appear or pass quickly.

guilty: Responsible for doing something bad or wrong.

hoax: Something meant to trick people.

information: Knowledge or facts about something.

journalist: Someone who works in journalism, or the job of collecting, writing, and editing news stories for news sources.

libel: The act of publishing a false statement that causes people to have a bad opinion of someone.

lure: To draw or cause someone to do something.

publisher: Someone in charge of publishing, or printing and presenting, things such as newspapers or books.

responsibility: Something you should do because it's right.

serious: Very important and worthy of attention, not funny.

skeptical: Having or sharing doubt about something, needing proof.

value: Something important, very helpful, or useful.

INDEX